You Define You

The 5-step playbook to authentic
self-rediscovery and keeping it for good

Lacey Delacroix

Lacey Delacroix

First Edition

ISBN: 979-8-218-55919-9

Copyright © 2024 Lacey Delacroix

All Rights Reserved.

Table Of Contents

Dear,	4
Step 1: Initial Awareness	7
Step 2: Inner Critic to Inner Confidant	23
Step 3: Divine Guides	36
Step 4: Triple Threat	51
Step 5: Plan with a Purpose	66
Sincerely,	71

Dear,

When I was 31 years old, I hit one of my darkest storms. I stared death in the eyes with a broken soul, beat up body, and a lifeless mind. This wasn't my first brush with death, although it felt the most real. Out of sheer desperation, I ended up creating a system, based off of my past experiences, to keep me going and stop life from taking me down. This was my turning point. I became so alive from this work; There was no going back.

The system I created is called The Pyramid of Authenticity. It is a five-step program which MUST be completed in sequence, within a suggested timeline of 60 days, or 8 weeks, which is best for the most successful results. The pyramid is representative of our being. The triangle is the strongest of all shapes. It relies on all three sides to work harmoniously to distribute its weight properly and can handle immense amounts of pressure. Our being, the triangle, is made up of the three sides: intellectual, spiritual, and physical. Within those three sides are the series of steps. Step one is the initial awareness and is allotted four weeks as it is the most crucial to build a solid foundation for the remaining four steps. Step two: Inner Critic to Inner Confidant, Step three: Divine Guides, Step Four: Triple Threat, and Step 5: Plan with a

Purpose are all allotted one week each. The point at the top of the pyramid is our highest self, or our authentic being. By living in this true essence, we are aligned with all we are in the purest form.

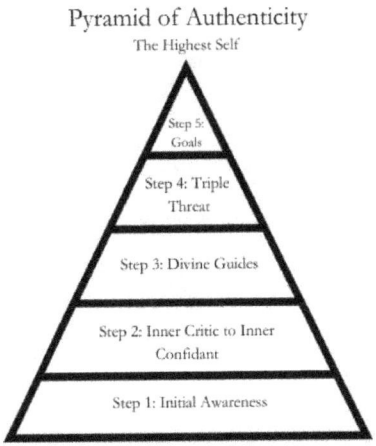

Pyramid of Authenticity

There are two distinct perspectives in viewing this playbook. The first perspective could be through the eyes of work by telling yourself everyday there is an objective to reach the end goal. The second perspective is through the eyes of a creative process by moving freely between self, thought, and feeling with a rhythm to get where you need to go. Either is perfectly acceptable, doable, and successful. If we do not make the mental distinction, the playbook may seen as stressful instead of with passion. Stress will weigh us down, while passion will light a fire in us to keep going. Throughout this process, the key to self-develop and be guided in the right direction is to retreat from the noise and grow silently. Working alone will increase the outcomes success by being rooted in deep reflection. Take this time to calmly and quietly get reacquainted with yourself.

The collection of stories I share transpires over the course of 16 years. Through each death and rebirth, I discovered along the way new insights to self-regeneration. The purpose in sharing these stories is twofold. First, I didn't come up with this playbook on a whim and have lived through the work myself. Second, I know there is a life waiting on the other side of whatever we may be going through. It doesn't matter what age we are or where we are in life, all of us at one point or another will get off-course. For those who are detached, stuck, lost, anxious, confused, depressed, angry, or simply needs a reset, this is for you. Let this playbook be your guide to self-rediscovery, self-awareness, and self-fulfillment. By implementing these steps and exercises, you will start to awaken the person sitting inside of you who deserves to come alive and stay alive.

Step 1: Initial Awareness

Duration: 4 Weeks

In my late teens, I woke up shivering in bed, drenched from cold sweats. There was a pain so deep clawing at all my muscles. I could barely walk or talk. This pain transcended my body and had taken over my mind and soul. The shutters next to my bed were cracked and the bright morning sun was warming every inch of my being. It was the hug I so deeply needed. I was in the throes of an opioid withdrawal. Just the day before, I told my parents I was selling my phone, turning off my number, deleting my social media, and staying home for the summer by myself to finally get clean. This wasn't my first time trying to kick the insidious pill. I had a few failed rehab attempts, all of which I went on my own accord. Although, through these grand failures, I realized nobody was going to save me from myself. If I wanted my life to change, it was up to me to make the change.

My essence was so broken from so many years of destruction; I didn't know which way was up, but I knew I was at the bottom. I was a full-fledged functioning addict for years. The high gave me the peace, control, and comfort I greatly craved. Eventually, no matter how high functioning you are in any area of life, there comes a point where you get sick and tired of feeling sick and tired. The functioning stops. Acutely aware of this, that first day of detoxing in my room felt different than all the other times I had tried to quit. I believe it was because of what my mom left by my bedside that morning before she went to work. It was a mini black notebook with a pen attached to the side of it. I was so angry and worn out, the first thing I did was scoff at the notebook and roll my eyes. As the day went on, I mustered up the energy to get out of bed and happen to walk by the mirror. That mirror was horrifying. I saw myself for what I was; A junkie who couldn't deal with life. I sat down on my bed feeling so defeated and lost. Feeling this way, I decided to pick up the notebook and wrote my very first entry, ever. "I can't believe this is me. I want to die." After writing those words, I shut the book. It became real. There was nowhere to run and hide. Nowhere to deflect and destruct. I had instantly become accountable. As a hard-shelled, ego-bound, thrill-seeking child, accountability was something I wasn't even remotely comfortable with. Being aware meant I had to do something about the mess I made of myself and the world around me. That notebook sat shut for a whole month. Something interesting happened though. First the first time in years, I didn't go back to the pills. What was different this time then all of the others? I had written it down. I got the initial anger, sadness, frustrations, and confusion out with just those two sentences. I believe those two sentences that afternoon saved my life.

I relied on this writing throughout that reclusive summer. I used it to carry me through when I was questioning everything. The words allowed me to become aware of everything going on in my life and where I was. It allowed me to see the shortcomings as well as the wins. As the years went on, the writing was on and off and nothing consistent. I thought, I'm doing great. I don't need writing. Only people who are lost and broken write. I couldn't have been more wrong. When were at our highs, we feel invincible. Nothing can take us down. But what if winter does come? Are you prepared? Have you been doing the inner work all along to be rooted and ready for whatever comes your way?

My darkest winter came when I was 31 years old. Between my teenage years and 31, I had many obstacles to overcome. In hindsight, these all prepared me for what I was going to experience this time around. A year prior to this dark winter, I started having stomach problems. Leading up to this, I had fixed almost 100% of the ailments I had accrued over the years. Although, my stomach kept getting worse. I had severe nausea, bloating, pain, acid reflux, and loss of appetite. My doctor and I did tests and found a giant gallstone causing bile issues, small intestinal bacterial overgrowth, pancreatic insufficiency, countless ulcers, H. Pylori, and parasites. My weight had gone from 120 pounds to 90 pounds. My doctor gave me a protocol to start killing off the pathogens and heal my stomach lining. Before I could start the protocol, I ended up in the hospital due to my gallbladder as its function had become essentially nonexistent. I left the hospital the next day with an appointment for surgery to remove my gallbladder. When I arrived for the surgery a few weeks later, I thought to myself, this would be a quick surgery and I'd be back to normal in a few weeks. Little did I know, I had a long road back to normalcy. I carry the same autoimmune disease as my mom that almost killed her a few years prior. I am now aware, the trauma of surgery can trigger a flare up. What I thought would be a week or two recovery time had turned into an over yearlong recovery. My vascular system became so inflamed and it effected every single organ of my body. My first few weeks of recovery were filled with severe pain which suits the diseases nickname, "the hurting disease". I had started to develop a very serious form of nausea, to the point, opening or moving my eyes would make me sick. Coming in contact with certain smells, textures, and bright colors made my stomach turn. I had to stay completely still in bed for about a month just to hold back any sickness. My stomach muscles and vocal cords became so weak, speaking was almost impossible. Touching my skin or showering became so painful, I'd cry at the slightest touch. My hands had reduced blood flow which inhibited their use for weeks. I developed an eye pain that was so severe I couldn't look at any type of screen or bright light for months. I had a migraine for over six months and couldn't move my neck or bend over without severe temporal pain. Any loud noise would send sharp jolts through my whole nervous system. My existence became pitch black. After all I had been through in life, I thought to myself, "This is what's going to take you out… how boring!"

    With my body so shattered, I wasn't sure I would physically be able to endure this time around. After a few months of being confined to a room, I finally had the strength to hold a pen and use my hands. The day this happened, my gratitude was indescribably high. My days became filled with Lego sets, crosswords, cryptograms, reading, scrabble, and writing. I asked my mom to buy a notebook, I simply couldn't go on anymore without getting down on paper what was going on in my head. When I started to write, it was multiple pages for multiple weeks. I had suppressed so much for so many years; The words poured out of me. When I faced the potential of death, my mind came alive. After a few weeks of unloading, my soul became much lighter. Slowly, the recovery process seemed less strenuous and my pain became more bearable. Dreams and goals started to present themselves again. I realized everything I was carrying inside of me all those years, was blocking me from the life I truly wanted to live. The focus to persevere and live authentically became inescapable.

Writing is the first step to keep yourself fully aware and grounded. When you start to get those words on the paper, deep transformation starts to happen over time. There is a feeling of being seen and heard. The notebook doesn't have an ulterior motive and the words won't lie to you. The pen will sit patiently waiting for you no matter how dark or bright your life. All of the patterns, cycles, and suppressed emotions and thoughts start to present themselves. The writing gives you a mirror; Seeing things for what they are and not what the mind, heart, or external influences have made them up to be. When you start questioning everything, answers will appear in the purest form. In some way, it becomes a cathartic spiritual practice. Family, friends, mentors, doctors, or therapists are all great for venting and sorting out thoughts. They also come with their version and perception of the situation. This can be good but not as an anchor. We are the anchor holding down our life. If we continually let the input of others dictate and be the only voice we hear, we will never know who we are but, they will. The writing process will allow you to start seeing the vision of who you are, what you truly want, and where you want to go.

I am the living proof of how terrifying those first few words can be. I am also living proof of how powerful and healing those words can be. You might be thinking, "This is easy for her to say. She wrote a book. Words and writing must have always come easy to her." This couldn't be further from the truth. All growing up, I actively avoided writing anything. Opening up my thoughts and emotions seemed foolish. I avoided it to the point I would happily take a zero in English class if it pertained to anything personal. Now, I always wonder where my life would be had I known the power of writing sooner.

Inevitably, detachment from our self will happen at some point in life. We can't recognize ourselves in the mirror, don't understand how we got in the situation we're in, or can feel immeasurably lost. Whether there are addictions, unfulfilling relationships, a mind-numbing career, an illness, losing someone, etc., we get detached simply because our mind tells us it's had enough. Enough of playing a role not meant for us anymore. My grandpa used to always say, "Depression is a deeply suppressed anger." I learned, our angers do not have the ability to lie. Therefore, our deep sadnesses, perplexations, or disconnects come from not wanting or fearing to see the truth. The mind starts to then drift away into unconsciousness. Contrary to what you may think, this unconscious detachment is what puts us on the path to set our minds free through rediscovery and defining who we are and what we want. Deflecting the truth will shave years off of your life, like it did mine. Facing the truth with courage sets you up to make a pointed lasting change.

Nothing will change in your life, if you don't make the change. Your last five years will look like the next five years if you don't stop, reflect, take inventory, and then take action. Here are the steps to regaining your consciousness.

1. Buy a pen or pencil and notebook. Phone and computer can work, although, I have found when our hand physically connects to the paper, a magic takes place. The emotions and thoughts appear to be more real and raw. Personally, I use an 8.5 x 11 notebook with a pen.

2. Find a time and place which is comfortable to you. It may be morning, noon, or night. This could be at home, your work, or during leisure time. Anytime and anywhere, you have quiet and safe environment to write. This is your sacred moment to be with yourself. Through observation, right when we wake up seems to be the best time to write. Our mind tends to be most honest, pure, and open to getting the words out.

3. I always keep it no more than 2-3 pages and less than 10 minutes. This is just an exercise to keep our thoughts, emotions, ideas, wants, needs, desires, and dreams in alignment and into a clear space. There are two routes you can take in starting your writing.

    a. The first route is to write freely. I have found this method best for the over-feelers. If you are a more fluid creative person, feel first, or don't like a rigid plan; This is for you. During your writing, staying in the present moment is best. There will be moments when the past and future show up, this is normal and okay.

Shed the weight you're dragging around. Let whatever comes up in that specific moment, out: Your emotions, your thoughts, your questions, your ideas, your needs, your desires, your fears, your excitements, your plans. etc. Let your fluidity guide your hand and let your hand guide your words.

b. The second route is a guided write. For the overthinkers or someone who doesn't know exactly where to start in their head or heart, this is for you. Generally, I see this format best for someone who is completely saturated from many years of suppressing.

    i. I call this guided write, the four-square method. I recommend it to anyone as a simple support and push to start letting the words out.

    ii. Take the sheet of paper in your notebook. Draw two lines, one horizontal and one vertical, down the center of the page. Each of the four squares represents a different question. An example of this is on pg. 16. You will answer each question freely as it comes to you in that moment. This is not an overthinking exercise; this is an initial stream of thought exercise. It may not make sense, that's okay. It may seem silly, that's okay. Release any judgements and just get the words out to unclog your system. Allow your thoughts to present themselves in the form of emotions, wants, needs, goals, and desires.

   c. At the end of your free write or guided write, use the last sentences to be what you are grateful for in the current moment and thanking yourself for something. I implement this because when we start expressing everything happening, we can lose sight of what we do have and what is going right in our life. The gratitude gives perspective and thanking ourselves gives us pause for self-appreciation. This simple action puts our mind and body on a positive trajectory for the day. There is evidence to support that we cannot be grateful and anxious, sad, or mad at the same time. Gratitude has also been shown to affect us physiologically as well. There is a study showing gratitude causes more blood flow to our heart which eventually leads up to our brain. A full heart is a healthy mind.

4. The last step is to store this notebook somewhere safe. This could be in your room, office, nightstand, a locked cabinet, under the mattress, etc. The notebook is for you and you only. No one else needs to be engaging themselves in your personal journey. If you are not in a safe situation, rip the paper out of your notebook when you are finished writing and discard. Your safety and well-being are more important than going back and reflecting.

Guided Write: Four Square Method Example

How am I feeling right now?	What is weighing heaviest on my mind right now?
What is one small goal I have for myself today?	What is one question I have for myself right now?

The first square is "How am I feeling right now?". When we start with the feeling in the current moment, an awareness starts to take over. It may be a single feeling or multiple feelings. We may be feeling happy, excited, lost, concerned, loved, or invisible. We may also be feeling nervous yet excited or content yet frustrated. There is no formula to how we feel. There is no right or wrong way to feel. The majority of us suppress what we truly feel for so long, we may not even know. Be patient with yourself and don't give up the first try. It may take a moment. The more aware we become, the easier the emotion will become. Staying in the present moment is vital for not drifting off into past and future feelings. This question is for right here, right now.

The second square is "What is weighing heaviest on my mind right now?". The previous question helps your emotional block. The emotional awareness will allow the mind to unlock and release what is truly happening. I have found when we don't start with the emotion, our mind will play its tricks to make up what we think should be going on. Usually, this squares answer is the one thing keeping us in complete unrest. It could be as minuet as, "I don't know how I am going to present in this meeting today." Or as monumental as "I don't know how we can make our marriage work anymore." Momentarily, you may feel heavier, having to get this out. For most, this is probably the first time having actually seen those words written down. The most important thing is to just let it out. Don't let this scare or stop you from your destiny of taking your power back and getting back to yourself again. The more you practice getting your thoughts out and sorted, the lighter you will become. You will start to think for yourself again.

The third square asks, "What is one small goal I have for myself today?" Taking inventory on a goal makes us start to think outside of ourselves. The goal pushes us to focus on something productive and accomplishing. The small daily goal could look like, "My goal for today is to get out of bed and try to eat something.", "My goal is to spend 15 minutes outside playing with my child", or "My goal is to print out a template for my new business plan." Working towards something is forward motion and removes us from the stuck position. When setting up a small goal every day, we start to train the mind for long-term goal setting which you will work on in step five.

The fourth question is "What is one question I have for myself right now?" Remember earlier when I mentioned, when we start to ask questions in our writing, the answers start to present themselves. This may or may not be immediate. Mine wasn't immediate and took time to strengthen. This question creates a deeper meaning to ourselves. You can ask any question in the world. You may ask yourself something like, "How have I let myself get in this situation?" or "Why am I picking the same partner over and over?" or "Am I truly happy in this career?" or "How can I be a better friend/parent/partner?" There are no dumb questions here. We will almost always have the answer when someone else is coming to us with their questions and problems. How come we don't have the answer for our own questions? The answer is our mind. Over time, I noticed we have the power to tap into different parts of our mind and find the answer. Sit in pure silence for a minute or two, ask yourself these questions and try to see if the answer comes to you. I think you will be surprised at truly how many answers we already know. For instance, if you ask "Why am I picking the same partner over and over?" Use your mind to tap into the relationship expert that is always there when your friends or family have a problem. Maybe this expert will have you make a list of all the traits you are picking and find out what is attracting you to this type of person. Maybe this expert will tell you it's something you're doing which is attracting that. If you ask, "Why is my new business failing?", Ask the seasoned entrepreneur in your mind, who is there for your friends and family every time they end up in a jam, "Why isn't my business reaching the heights I thought it would?" There is a good chance that entrepreneur will know exactly why your business isn't reach the goals you thought it would. This idea of tapping into different identities has helped me profoundly. Sometimes, the answers we are always searching for are within us the whole time.

If you want lasting change, writing every single day is the most beneficial. I now do not miss one day of writing. If I am at a high point in my life, I write. If I am at a low point in my life, I write. If I am on vacation, I write. If I am incredibly tired or busy, I write. For the guided writers, eventually, turning to a free write everyday would be ideal. The free write is the next step in you taking the reins of your own life. When you make this transition, start applying the question, "why?" to everything you're thinking or feeling. This is important because it will start putting a reason and accountability behind what is making you feel or think a certain way. With this accountability, you will start to become the guide of your own emotions, thoughts, questions, goals, etc. Our life is changing every second, of every day, of every year. If we don't stay current with ourselves, we will stay stuck.

There will be days where you forget to write or get too busy to write. Maybe you will only write a few sentences. Maybe you'll make a few mistakes along the way. Please know, these faults do not define you. Actually, it's the opposite. Your faults only allow you to learn more about yourself in which you can use to your advantage. It means you're actually trying, which is already placing you ahead of most. Perfection doesn't exist, don't bother. Every day is new day to refresh and build upon what's behind us. I always say, speak to yourself as if you are speaking to a child. Make the conscious effort and choice to be kind, loving, patient, and supportive of yourself. There will be a point in the writing process where the inner critic, your fault-finder, will appear. We all have one. The critic will say, "This isn't long enough. This is too short. You don't really think that, do you? This isn't grammatically correct. Are you sure you feel this way? Are you being too sensitive?" Anytime you have this critic come around, tell it to go away. This is the beginning of your personal work and journey. It doesn't control you; You control it.

For both guided writers and free writers, before going to step two, try to write for four weeks. I have worked with shorter and longer times and have found 30 days to be a good jump point. Over the course of the four weeks, I have a simple task for each week. Each task serves its own purpose for you to dig deeper into yourself and will come in handy during the next four steps of the book.

Week 1 Task: I start the first week off with one of my favorite exercises. I call this exercise ten lives. It is very playful and hopeful activity. When we are children, the world is so full of curiosities. Anything is possible. As we grow older, we lose this freedom and sense of wonder. Life tends to put up guard rails and say we can't do certain things or be a certain person because it doesn't fall in line with society. This is not true. We can be whoever we want to be. In this week's exercise, make a list of ten lives you have always wanted to live. For example: artist, cowboy, surfer, editor, engineer, florist, photographer, mountain biker, chef, mechanic, seamstress, etc. During this first month of writing, you will choose one of the ten lives and live it. For instance, if you want to be an artist, take an art class. If you want to be a mountain biker, rent a bike and go on a trail or join a mountain biking group and have them mentor you. If you've always wanted to be a chef, take a cooking class. The goal of this is to show you how fully capable you are of being the person you have dreamed of and opening yourself up to new possibilities.

Week 2 Task: During this second week, make a list of five strengths and five weaknesses you have. Being able to show up more effectively for yourself and others is harder if you're not even sure what your strong and weak points are. I have always believed knowing the bad is just as important as knowing the good. Our weaknesses point out what we can work on and how to communicate to ourselves and others where we are lacking. Our strengths highlight where we can be of service to ourselves and others. Sometimes, our strength can act as weakness and vis versa. If this is the case, try to put this particular trait in the category where it has a stronger effect on your life. Staying current with our strengths and weaknesses allow us to keep our world a well-oiled machine by communicating and moving more efficiently. This list will be a good reference for step five.

Week 3 Task: I call this week the identity block. As life happens, humans log each daily experience whether good or bad. The good side of this, our mind knows there are great things out there happening and experiencing good is possible. The bad side of this, humans tend to hold onto the negative ones more often and allow them to be their limiting beliefs. Some examples are, "I am not smart enough for the promotion." "I am not pretty and will never attract the partner I want." "I am so weak and always let people walk all over me." Most people have numerous limiting beliefs. For this exercise, write down only five of your identity blocks. The biggest ones that are holding you back from pursing the person you want to be and the life you want to have. We will use this in step two.

Week 4 Task: The forgiveness week. I have found this exercise the most critical in moving forward wholly and authentically. During this week, write down ten pieces from your life to forgive. This exercise is forgiving others, as well as yourself. Life is not a fair game, but forgiveness is. Nothing is too big, too small, too stupid, too silly, too light, too dark, too serious, too funny, too old, or too new to put on that list. Writing this down is one small step closer to a bigger vision of mental, emotional, physical, and spiritual freedom. Keep this list as you will need it during step 3 where I will show you have to move through this unnecessary weight.

Step 2: Inner Critic to Inner Confidant

Duration: 1 Week

As we continue our daily writing, the next step to learn and implement is the intellectual side of the pyramid, our inner voice. This is the voice speaking to us all the time. It has the power to push us in the right direction or hold us back. All of our life decisions are based off of this one voice. When we start writing, our deep suppressions may start to show up. These suppressions usually highlight how long we have allowed friends, life experiences, family, work, or any outside influence dictate our inner voice. These are called identity blocks and they start to consume the mind and inhibit any type of growth. When we tell ourselves the same story over and over, our life will reflect that story. We become what we think. The more attention we give the negative inner critic, the more we become this person. I will show how to take the inner critic we all have and make it our inner confidant. If we don't make sure to take care of our subconscious, someone will do it for us.

During my early school years is where I believe the start of my inner critic really started to take shape. I had numerous teachers who were very insecure and let the questions and push back from a child make them act poorly. My curious free-spirit was clearly too much for them to handle. They said things I don't think any child should ever hear. Even though I had the grit to push back, I still let the words get to my head. I internalized everything. My inner critic was saying, "I am not good enough. I am not smart enough. I am not capable enough." I gave the power to everyone around me to dictate what to think, how to act, and what to feel. I ended up building a very tall, impenetrable wall. This wall pushed out all of the bad, as well as, all the good happening around me. Subsequently, a very destructive, numb, and shallow person was created. I didn't understand at the time that my voice was lacking which is another way of saying I didn't love myself. We don't hurt ourselves or others when we love ourselves first.

  The experiences from these years cultivated a very guarded perspective of the world. With the high level of distrust I garnered, only a few of my connections were completely genuine. When I was 16, I met someone who would eventually become my boyfriend. He was a lot of fun, spontaneous, confident, and we laughed all the time. We could count on each other, open up without judgement, and let down our walls. There was a rough edge from his upbringing that kept a separation from him and the outside world. We saw eye to eye on this external world and had a deep understanding of what the other was thinking or feeling. In most relationships, this understanding is a good thing and brings people closer together. It is also the one thing that can tear people apart faster than you can blink. Eventually, alcohol and drugs started to take precedence in our relationship. Quickly, the drugs took a tighter hold. Before we knew it, we had become two people neither of us could recognize. What was once a safe space, filled with fun and love, was now a battlefield. Back and forth, we were throwing grenades and seeing how badly we could damage the other person. The last night we saw each other, I raised my white flag. My mind and body had slowly withered and simply couldn't take the hits anymore. From complete disbelief of that last night's transpiring events, I thought, "How could someone I loved do this to me? Is this love? Maybe this is something I deserved?" I absorbed every action and word from that last night and it stayed with me for years. I lost trust. I lost faith. I had lost it all.

Ultimately, this led to me making a change in my relationships. My intellect took over and dictated the control I had to never let anyone do this to me again. My inner narrator said, "I need to be in control of everything. Don't ever let your guard again, otherwise, that night will happen all over again." The following romantic relationships were always very kind, supportive, and fun. Yet, they were always short lived and never fully open or real. There was always something missing. Eventually, I decided to take a step back and find out what was wrong. After many years of being alone and thinking endlessly, I realized, my inner critic wasn't accurate or authentic. What was missing from these relationships was me. I did not have an inner confidant supporting, loving, and guiding me. One of the first things to start suffering when there is a damaged inner voice at play, is the connections we have with the outside world. Our relationships are generally a direct reflection of the one we have with ourselves. What I didn't understand at that time, we can only love others as deeply as we love ourselves. To love ourselves and others, we have to incorporate a loving and strong inner confidant to rely on every minute of our lives.

My first experience with my inner confidant work was with overcoming my opiate addiction. When I wanted to get sober, I knew had I had to change my mind. After the initial withdraw and slowly coming back to, I started to speak to myself. Through those summer months, I told myself every day, "I am not an addict and this will not be the rest of my life." Never once did I count how many days I was sober. Never once did I think about going back to old habits. And never once did I believe myself to be wrong. This was because I did not sit in the identity of an addict. The days, old habits, and shame didn't matter. My identity is what mattered. The daily writing during those months helped me release any uneasiness which led me to be become lighter and believe stronger in my thinking. If I were to sit in the old identity of being an addict, my woe is me attitude and safety net of excuses would only continue to take the lead. With the new identity, my life took a new path.

Years later at 25 years old, I started to develop severe health issues. My body started to burn to the point of tears, my joints were getting stuck, severe chemical and food sensitivities started to develop, and countless other symptoms were appearing daily. Out of all of these symptoms, the most prominent one was OCD, or obsessive-compulsive disorder. Most of the health issues were manageable but this OCD took me down, hard. I thought from the years of deep stress from taking care of both my parents, it was just a fluke and would pass. What started as frequent hand washing quickly transpired into intrusive thoughts, irrational fears, and superstitions. It became so bad I couldn't physically be alone anymore. My showers became 3 hours long. And nothing felt "just right". These were very dark times and a pivotal moment in which I started to *really* develop my inner voice. I started to visit numerous doctors and therapists to see if they had any ideas on why this was happening. I was told every time, this is just in my mind and nothing could help. In turn, I kept telling myself, "I guess this is true. There is no answer and I will be like this forever. There is no hope." By continually repeating this to myself, I kept attracting this in my life. Deep down, I knew something wasn't right. This is when I started to listen to myself. Logically, I thought, if I am getting continually worse than something must be triggering this. One night, two hours into one of these OCD showers, I had started to shake and cry I was so mentally and physically exhausted. I had used a whole bottle of soap, shampoo, conditioner, and toothpaste. I couldn't stand anymore. I squatted in the shower and just cried. I let the water wash away my tears with my eyes closed. All of the sudden, inside my head there was a voice, it said, "Lacey you are tough, you are bright, and you can find the answer to this. There is hope. Don't give up." I couldn't believe it. It was one of those lightbulb moments. I had never said those words to myself before and it gave me an instant power I had never felt. After this happened, I stood up and turned off the water. I made up my mind. I thought, "I am right. I am tough, I am bright, and I can find the answer." What I was being told didn't need to define the rest of my life. I dried off and went to bed that night vibrating from sheer burnout.

The next morning, I woke up and opened up my computer. I researched for days and weeks, deep diving for information relentlessly,

"What causes OCD? How can I cure my OCD? What triggers OCD?" The information I found was mind blowing. Environmental toxins, heavy metals, viruses, traumas, toxic mold, hormones, inflammation, allergies, and much more can cause OCD. Through research, a doctor out of Pheonix, Arizona came my way. She had tremendous experience working with patients with mold toxicity, breast implant illness, Lyme's disease, neurological issues, and gastrointestinal issues. I was in such a deeply anxious state during this time; The idea of driving to Arizona was very daunting. Before I called to make the appointment, I noticed my inner voice come back. "Lacey, you are strong. You can make this appointment and you can drive to Arizona. It might save your life." Those words instantly changed my internal state and gave me a boost to move forward. In retrospect, it was the one appointment that did save my life. Our first appointment was almost three hours long. She asked me questions no other doctor or therapist had ever asked. She listened to every single word I said and respected everything I had to say. She never doubted or questioned my thoughts and never pushed back. Her empathy was astounding and this was a new feeling to me. It didn't feel real. After many roadblocks and push back from doctors, I was finally shown the path with ease. When I started to change the voice inside, the outside world started to change with it.

    After our extensive appointment and countless testing, I had toxic mold in my body, heavy metals, severe hormone imbalance, food allergies, and extreme toxicity from my ruptured breast implants. The critic in me didn't want to believe it. I wanted to protect myself so badly from anything bad happening. My inner voice kicked in once again in that hotel room in Arizona. "Lacey, you are the leader in your life, no one else. Use the knowledge you have now and the plan you have now, to heal." This was all I needed to hear from myself. I let my guard down. I took the holistic herbal protocol we worked on together and started detoxing the mold and metals, stopped taking my birth control, stopped drinking out of BPA water bottles, completely changed my diet, worked on healing old wounds, and had my ruptured breast implants removed. This was a slow and arduous process. Over time though, I started to get better. It was a complete miracle. After a few years, the mold was undetectable, metals were at normal levels, hormones leveled out, the majority of my symptoms were gone, and I was able to work through my past. The OCD which had plagued me and made me question life, was eventually nonexistent. If it wasn't for that inner voice, I don't think I would have ever allowed myself the joy of letting my guard down, healing, and the courage to trust again.

When my darkest storm came at 31, I didn't realize this voice would become one of the tools I needed most. On the day of my gallbladder surgery, I was a little concerned as I weighed 90 pounds. I was so thin and malnourished and didn't know if my body would make it through. Tears couldn't stop rolling down my face and the hospital staff did their best to comfort me. They were about to wheel me into the operating room but I was not in a good headspace. I knew this mindset would not serve me well. I laid there, closed my eyes, and drowned out all the commotion around me. I took a few moments and said, "Lacey you cannot go into surgery with this attitude otherwise you will not make it. Your weight will not affect the outcome of this surgery, only your outlook and attitude will. You are healthy, strong, and will be just fine." I opened my eyes with no tears on my face. I looked at my mom and said, "Okay, I'm ready." They wheeled me off for the surgery. Speaking this way to myself gave me hope. In that exact moment, I learned the path to inner peace and comfort can only come from one place, the voice within.

For that first month of recovery, the voice that spoke to me was everything. My physical voice was too weak to use, all I had was my inner voice. I said to myself continuously for days, "This is not taking me down. I am focused on healing." Over that first month of recovery, I had lost even more weight and was about 85 pounds. Due to my severe nausea, I couldn't eat or drink much. My system started having allergic reactions to all foods with the exception of about five items. When I saw how thin I was in the mirror, I couldn't even recognize myself. I jumped to my inner voice immediately and said to myself, "I am now stronger than I could have ever imagined. I am healed. I am healed. I am healed." and I would hold up my twiggy arms in the mirror flexing them. Physically, I would feel the feeling of strength and let it marinate in every cell of my body. I did this every day all day in my head and out loud. Slowly, this voice changed my view of the current situation. I was no longer a victim. I was the leader and not going to let it take me down like other events in the past. Every single day became easier and easier. Every day I became stronger and soulfully lighter. My inner word shifted the whole reality. Even though I was still very unwell, I was healed. I was the leader and directing my reality where to go.

Our inner director is a force to reckon with when the energy is harnessed correctly. Our perception is molded by this voice and we must be careful how we use it. It can make us carry the weight of the world on our shoulders or it can take the weight of the world off our shoulders. Whenever we are down, we tend to start grabbing at everything around us to feel complete. We think this person, this bottle of wine, this vacation, this project, etc. will make us whole; It won't. Our inner state is what will make us whole. Our life will be better, when we become better. Our subconscious mind listens intently to our conscious mind. Thus, the self-image is created.

There is an exercise that helps reawaken our intellectual and emotional state which I like to start with before any deeper work. When life sweeps us up, getting lost in everyone's world around us and losing sight of what brings us joy is unavoidable. In order to rekindle the healthy relationship and joys we have with ourselves, grab a sheet of paper and write down five activities you truly love and miss doing. These activities have to be achievable in some form and something you haven't done in ages. Some examples could be a dinner party with friends, reading a book while people watching at the local coffee shop, strolling the local gardens, yearly fishing trips with the boys, yearly girls' trip, painting on a canvas again, etc. Choose one activity and make it an immediate priority to achieve. There is a sense of freedom, joy, and satisfaction once it is accomplished. Our mind and heart become opened up and ready to receive again.

In step one, you worked on an exercise called identity block. This was the limiting beliefs about yourself, which stops you from becoming the person you desire. If you change the story you tell yourself, you will change the world within and the world around. Here is how to change your story:

1. From the identity block list you made in step one, pick one belief that is jumping out the most.
2. Take a sheet of paper. Write down the exact opposite of the one identity block belief you chose.
3. Make this new identity in present tense as if you have already obtained it. You're turning the old, wrong, and washed-up identity block into an abundant affirmation rooted in belief, love, care, and determination. Here are a few examples:

Old Identity Block	New Identity Affirmation
I am not smart enough for the promotion.	I have more than enough intellect, perseverance, and resiliency to obtain the promotion. I add an ample amount of value which is showcased through my accomplishments.
I am not pretty and will never attract the partner I want.	I am beautiful inside and out. I attract the right person at the right time. We see eye to eye on the beauty each of us carry with tenderness and poise.
I am so weak and always let people walk all over me.	I am rooted and sturdy like an ox. I speak up for myself gracefully while still being of service to myself and others.

4. You will take this paper with you in your notebook, purse, backpack, desk, etc. and read it every single day, multiple times a day. This is your affirmation for the remainder of the playbook. After this playbook, apply this process to all your identity blocks. Personally, I use my affirmations every single day.

At first, it feels totally nuts saying this new story. For such a long time, you were telling yourself the untrue version. The imposter can seem very real during this time. Eventually though, these words will become the new reality. You will start to match the frequency of which you desire to be. Don't believe me? Look at where your inner critic has gotten you thus far.

The next step is saying the affirmations out loud with a physical component. When we say the affirmation out loud our brain starts logging it differently. By taking physical action, it changes our physical state by harnessing the feeling responsible for creating the self-image. For so many years, I was in my head with my affirmations, which still continues today. The real change came when I stood in front of that mirror at 85 pounds and held my arms up like I was in a bodybuilding competition saying to myself out loud "I am stronger than I could have ever imagined. I am healed. I am healed. I am healed." I put my arms up to feel the sensation of being strong. I would say it, believe it, and feel it deeply. I realized in this exact moment, when we add a physical layer to the affirmation it makes us unstoppable. You will need to find the right physical gesture to accompany your new identity affirmation while saying it out loud.

Here are a few ideas for the previous examples:

New Identity Affirmation Spoken out loud	Accompanying Physical Gesture
I have more than enough intellect, perseverance, and resiliency to obtain the promotion. I add an ample amount of value which is showcased through my accomplishments.	Lightly tap each side of your brain to feel the intelligence you carry.
I am beautiful inside and out. I attract the right person at the right time. We see eye to eye on the beauty each of us carry with tenderness and poise.	Hold your hand over your heart to feel the pure love you have for yourself and others.
"I am rooted and sturdy like an ox. I speak up for myself gracefully while still being of service to myself and others."	Hold your hands on your hips like a superhero, both feet on the ground and back straight up holding the feeling of being confident and grounded.

By the end of this step, the most prominent behavior I've witnessed is people hitting the wall of judgement. It could be a feeling of judgement from yourself or others. If you hit this wall, try to remind yourself, the mind will create any scenario to support the self-doubt you have on yourself. You will come to realize the imagination is the biggest culprit on assumptions of judgement. If the judgement is consuming you, create a new affirmation drowning out the judgement. For example: "Judgement does not own me. There is only one of me. I am grateful and proud of the person I am now and the person I am becoming." The physical movement you may want to try is jumping up and down while saying it to change your state from nervous of judgement to excited for the judgment as it can only make you stronger. Eventually, this will become reality. Through all my ups and downs, I was under no illusion of what my current situations were. I was also very aware that if I didn't change the way I was thinking, my current situation would only continue me down the same unwanted path. The second you hear your old identity blocks come to the forefront, repeat your new identities over and over, louder and louder. Becoming victorious and unstoppable in the true spirit of self is through the powerful inner confidant.

Step 3: Divine Guides

Duration: 1 Week

The next side of the triangle we will work on is the spiritual side. Out of the three sides, this one is usually the most neglected. Spirituality is such an abstract idea and for many incredibly hard to grasp. Turning this infinite concept into one finite idea has been debated and investigated for thousands of years. My goal is to not push you into one way of thinking or pigeonhole spirituality to one single idea. I want you to use your writing and inner voice to be the guide of what you believe is the right path. It is harder to be truly aligned with oneself when our system is bombarded with all the daily battles, all the past experiences, and all the unnecessary weight dragging the us down. This step is where I learned the process of consciously releasing and unconsciously relying.

When I was 23 years old, I had moved back to my parent's house. It was a very exciting time as I had a job waiting for me abroad. My focus was on making sure my parents health and life were in order before leaving. Every day from dusk until dawn, we were swamped making sure all was good and well before I left. With the stress of it all weighing heavy on me, I needed a break. I called up a friend and headed out to get dinner and a drink. What was supposed to be a simple night out of disengaging and resetting my mind turned into a life changing event. My friend and I went to dinner and after, we went across the way to meet up with friends for a drink. I thought to myself at the time, its only one drink and we'll head home. The next morning, I opened my eyes from the sun blaring through huge windows, in a home I didn't recognize. The initial, anxious thought was, "Where am I and where are my friends?" When I looked around, I saw one of my friends on the other couch across from me which was a sigh of relief. We were both "okay". I woke her up and we immediately left. As we walked out of the house, we realized we were right across the street from that particular bar. We hopped in the car and drove home trying to piece together the night. We didn't remember anything from that night and later found out, neither did anyone from our group. As the day went on, I realized I was not feeling right. I was shaky, I couldn't find my words for things, and I couldn't find it in me to eat or drink anything. When night came, I asked my mom if she would sleep with me because I wasn't feeling well. In the middle of the night, I woke up not being able to breathe, my body dripping in sweat, my heart rapidly racing, and my vision had gone black with white flashes everywhere. The walls came in on me and it felt like my soul left my body. After an hour of this, I closed my eyes on the bed with the white flashes still blinding me. Eventually, I was able to get back to sleep for an hour or two. When I woke back up, I didn't feel in reality. I had completely disassociated. I was in my body but viewing the world from a different angle. I spoke to my doctor later that day and came to the conclusion there was more than alcohol in my system and my mind was protecting me from the distress of transpiring events. Over the course of that week, my condition only worsened. I could barely think and was increasingly disconnected. I stopped talking and started observing. Eventually, I had to reach out to the company overseas and say I cannot make it anymore due to my health. I had to cancel all the projects I was working on with my parents. My entire world stopped. My last dance with alcohol was that night and I've never looked back.

    Following this life-altering week, the first thing I did was pull out a journal. It was a brown leather-bound journal with an embossed mandala on it. One of my past love interests from abroad had gifted it when he visited and I greatly cherished its meaning. It gave me the loving solace I was seeking. The first thing I wrote in the journal was the noble eightfold path of Buddhism. This path gave me something other than the one I was currently on which was heavily riddled with feelings of distrust, violation, and disgust. I was so lost and shaken to the core; I just needed something to grab onto. Prior to this, I had taken a few world religion courses in college. During these courses, Buddhism always resonated with me the most. Deep down, I knew if I wanted to survive this seismic shift of reality, I needed to find an answer. I needed to slow down and expand my consciousness, reach for something greater than myself, and start believing there was a reason for all of this. That's exactly what I did. I kept to myself and didn't talk to any friends or family during those months of reflection, healing, and learning. I started yoga to process the duality of wanting peace but living in complete internal disarray. I signed up for the English Buddhism classes at my local temple for clarity and direction. My energy went to learning on letting the anger, sadness, anxiety, and confusion pass by. I was also learning to let the joys and daily wins pass. This was a new feeling I had never felt before. For the first time, I wasn't allowing myself to get wrapped up in all the chaos. By walking the path of Buddhism, it helped me make right of what wrong had transpired. After many months of this work, my mind lifted and my body was freer. There was a glimmer of hope.

A few years later, when I was 25, I had a meeting with one of my spiritual teachers. Our meeting came on the heels of my dad's passing and during the roughest phase of my OCD. My life force was fading and I was strongly considering becoming a monk. My Buddhism had gone by the wayside and I was soullessly searching for any answer I could find. During this time, *finding* the stillness didn't seem attainable. When my spiritual teacher saw me, she could see how dark I was. She sat me down and actually yelled at me, "Lacey, you are only focused on the yellow. Don't you see?" I was taken aback as she never raised her voice. She then said, "You are so focused on this one color. You need to take a step back and look at this huge portrait that is in front of you. Wake up." Much to my dismay, she was right. I was so focused on myself and what was going wrong. I lost sight of all the good that was around me. I wasn't leaning into an infinite source, at all. I wasn't letting go of my battles and carried that weight everywhere with me. I wasn't honoring the little moments of life that were lifting me up and carrying me through. She recommended reading two books and these two books changed my views on spirituality completely. I didn't really understand the component of fostering a relationship with infinite source and *being* the stillness. After digesting this newfound information, I got still with myself. Whatever I was running from would only continue to chase me. I started expanding and believing in higher powers other than Buddhism. Over the course of a few years, I studied Christianity, Hinduism, philosophers, nature, and Taoism. My goal was to gain as much insight in order to define a well-rounded relationship with divine source.

Through observation, I tend to see more self-loathing, self-destructive, and self-absorbed behaviors when someone is spiritually bankrupt. Our ability to believe takes us out of "me" and into "we". Believing and prayer pushes us out of our physical and intellectual worlds and into the spiritual world. It reminds us we are not alone. Resiliency comes easier. Answers come easier. Leading with love comes easier. Believing starts to show, it will all be *okay*.

When I was recovering from my surgery and wasn't sure if I was going to be alive each morning, I found spirituality jumping into my life again. I was in so much pain, physically, mentally, and emotionally, all I could think, "Is there a higher power or a force for good if I am this sick?" Even though I remained still and grounded, this narrow-minded spiritual thinking of sickness only brought more sickness. One day, I closed my eyes for a few hours laying on the bed in complete silence. The darkness in my eyes started to show all the brightness in my life. I envisioned a God of light, a God of love, and a God of pure healing powers touching all my blood vessels. I imagined little angels flying around my body taking a needle and thread sowing all the damaged vessels back to their original state. Each day, while confined to the bed and house, for a few hours' morning and night, I closed my eyes and had these beings heal every part of my body. Slowly, hour by hour, I could actually feel the healing take place. Call it quackery, call it divine intelligence, or call it a miracle; For me, it was real. I started to believe so deeply that instead of something working against me, something was working with me. It was working with me all along; I just needed to believe it. What was missing was actually feeling and embracing its help. A true relationship. If you quiet your mind and start to feel all is working harmoniously in your favor, everything starts becoming in your favor.

After a few months at home recovering from the flare up, I was genuinely craving people, plants, animals, sounds, and the smells of the world. I was still practicing this vision work of being healed by some power I still can't explain. I did start to feel off balance though. I was feeling spiritually empty. This is when nature became my next belief system. I started to play YouTube videos of people hiking on trails, ariel views of different parts of the world, and timelapses of sunrises and sunsets. This carried my soul to a dimension it desperately desired. I believed so strongly that the mountains, water, rocks, sky, trees, animals, and soil would be my guiding force of light, health and love. I printed pictures from nature and different location around the world that were soothing my soul and put them next to me every day. I stared at them and prayed to them allowing them to do the spiritual work. I then started to read poetry and listen to classical music. Those became my next soul supporters. I believed they had the power that transcended the world I was living in and be the guides to a higher state. And this is exactly what they did. When you start to believe something has the power to guide wholly- that is so bright, so loving, so powerful- the world suddenly starts to open up in a way it never did before. The chains get broken and the soul starts to become a little freer. My multidimensional spiritual connections taught me that anything can become a belief system. We are only confined to the walls our mind creates.

Before jumping to the divine guides work this week, I have a fun activity. Take a piece of paper and fill it up with pictures of people, places, or objects that give you the sense of peace the soul desires. These pictures are spiritually transcending. They take you to another world where true love, protection, peace, and support consumes you. For example: beaches, mountains, flowers, books, sculptures, architecture, music, family, a city, a country, a landmark, Buddha, Jesus, dogs, cats, oil paintings, Aristotle, churches, seashells, etc. Anything under the sun. Either print out the collage you make or glue the pictures on a single piece of paper. Each day this week and through to the end of the playbook, take a moment to look at these pictures and believe they have the power to fill your soul up with all the love, protection, health, guidance, light, and peace. The reason I start with this exercise is because it generates a feeling that is needed to connect with source.

Most of us carry a notion that believing in something has to look a certain way. I started to refuse this idea because it only led to my own suffering. There is a point in this chapter, where I see a lot of people become defined by preconceived notions or past experiences which may present itself in ways of feeling spiritually overwhelmed or detached. I once heard someone say, "I don't believe in anything. Spirituality is complete nonsense." Their very next sentence was, "But when I am with my dog, I believe they have the deepest unconditional love that bears the weight of all my worries. It all goes away when I am with my pet." Even though this person thought they didn't believe in a certain religion or higher power, they actually did. Their pet was their guiding force of love and light. Give yourself the permission to accept and release all the sufferings and explore different ideas, deeper meanings, and soulful connections. Now is a good time to lean heavily into your inner confidant for the courage to become enlightened. Remind yourself this- "I am on a journey of discovery. I am letting the uncertainty pass freely while I continue the forward motion of become free. Free through the belief that life is filled with an abundant source of light and love that is ready to guide me wholly."

Through all my ups and downs, I've had to shed a piece of me each time I trekked forward. Any time we go through a process of re-evaluation and growth there will be moments of death. Death of mind, death of emotions, death of spirit, death of relationships, death of life eras, or death of attachments. During the grieving process is where I always debated going back to the old self because it was "easier". Don't fall into this tricky trap. It may seem easier to stay in the comfort zone although, life will only continue to get harder. It will be harder as your discontentment will only grow larger. On the other side of this death though, is a rebirth. A rebirth of thinking, feeling, seeing, and doing. Leading by your newfound self will bring an end to unwanted cycles and a wisdom you would have never had if you hadn't stayed the course. Grieving the self is sometimes a very spiritual practice. During these transitory moments, is where I have seen myself and others gain a different lens to the idea of *let go and let God*. Keep your grievances in mind for this upcoming exercise.

During step one, you were to write down ten pieces from your life to forgive. This could come in the form of forgiving yourself or others.

I learned from one of my mentors, when we don't forgive and still carry the ill towards others or ourselves, we will attract more of that into our life. If we keep it in and run with it, it will continue to chase us. In short, the internal suffering will create more external suffering. By making a conscious effort to remain grounded, stop running, and release these negativities, a sense of freedom and power presents itself. Sometimes, people will end up in the same precarious situations over and over because they carry a blame list instead of a forgiveness list. Take every single piece from your forgiveness list and pray for forgiveness every day through to the end of this playbook including any grievances you may carry. Pray for the burden and resentments to wash away. Pray for the good will to come to you and others. Pray this negative energy is released from your being. For each line of forgiveness, simply say, "I pray for the release and forgiveness of XYZ. I am ready to move on completely and I pray this is resolved for the highest good." I have found this to be a great way to start priming the mind to be open and willing to the power of prayer. The soul can only handle holding onto so much for so long. Becoming the best version of yourself is to seek the highest form of yourself and forgiveness belongs with you at the top.

If you already practice a particular form of spirituality, that is wonderful. You are already ahead of most. Please consider attending a class or reading a book on a different form such as another religion or a philosopher. This action forces you into a different perspective. That perspective allows for more empathy of others situations, better understanding of yours and others thoughts, and deeper awareness of where you stand with your own belief system. When we stick with one point of view, were stuck in perception. I find perception to one of the biggest sticking points for growth. Perception will lead to a stunted life because life will only go as far as your single view. We have become a society that doesn't question anymore. What is a life without question? It is a life without answers. Let my journey be your permission to question, seek answers, and see spirituality can be an ever-changing path depending on the season of life you may experiencing.

Before learning how to connect with source, it is important to find out what our spirituality is in this exact moment and the daily writing is a great place to explore this idea. Divine source can present itself in many facets. The first being a religion like Christianity, Buddhism, Islamic, Catholicism, Judaism, etc. The second is in the form of nature such as the trees, mountains, oceans, sky, plants, animals, or birds. Sometimes an activity for us can be a spiritual practice such as long walks, being with our pet, painting, sculpting, hiking, reading philosophy, surfing, or meditating. Lastly, there is an all-encompassing infinite intelligence in the form of Universe, God, angels or a loved one whose passed. Sometimes your God is nature, surfing, or the sky. The list is endless and non-linear. There is no right or wrong- only your perspective. Take a moment and through the initial thought, find what brings a force of light to your world. True divine source will not rattle you. True divine source will not make you question everything. True divine source will give you the space, patience, love, support, guidance, and softness the soul longs for. Here are the steps to start cultivating connection:

1. Start by finding a quiet moment. A great place to start is right after your daily writing or when you are engaging in the activity that you view as your spiritual guide such as hiking, painting, etc.
2. Reflect on your daily writing and see what feelings and thoughts are heaviest at that moment. Choose one of these to pray over.
3. Close your eyes and get still. Start to fill your heart up with the feeling of pure love.
4. In your mind, or out loud, start to speak with your source over your single prayer. Feel the source with you. Here are some examples of how I speak with divine throughout the day:
    a. When my health is starting to impede my daily living, I say, "Angels, I pray for the release of this physical pain and know you are here helping heal every cell in my body. I am grateful for your strength and wisdom to carry on with ease and grace."
    b. When I am feeling stressed out and lost, I say, "God, I know you are walking with me every step of the way and I am grateful to you for the steady pace you give me. Please continue highlighting the best path for me to take of the highest good. Let me be the vessel of your light and love."
    c. When I am feeling overwhelmed with gratitude, I say, "Universe, I cannot believe how lucky I am to be alive. Thank you so much for always bringing such great things to my life. My gratitude for your support and love is overwhelming. Thank you."

d. When I am feeling disconnected, I got outside and look at nature, I say, "Nature, your force of love is so strong in my life. You always have the right answers in the right time. Thank you for showing me the way of the highest good and reconnecting me as deemed necessary in your time."

e. When I am intellectually needing support, I will go to my philosophy books, I say, "Philosophers, thank you for always being a grounding force of pure wisdom. Please illuminate me with your words to be reminded of who I am and how I should proceed."

f. When I am lacking affection, I say, "My dearest dog, I pray my heart is as unconditional and eternally loving as you to myself and others. Thank you for always being the warmth that comforts my soul and giving me the freedom to be myself."

g. When I am on my daily walks with my dog and looking to be protected, I say "Universe, please protect us on this walk and show us the way. Thank you so much for shielding us with your light."

h. When I am looking for a parking spot during the hectic holidays and becoming anxiety ridden, I say, "God, the perfect spot will open up in your perfect timing. Thank you so much for guiding me with your love to the perfect place, safely."

i. When I am feeling creatively empty, I say, "Artists, please let your creativity wash over me and allow me to create with higher purpose as you have. I am eternally grateful for the emotional support you give my life."

5. In the beginning of fostering a relationship with your divine, try to keep the initial conversation short. One or two sentences is sufficient. If the prayers are too long winded in the beginning, the mind starts to lose focus. This should only be a few seconds of your time.

6. Practice your single prayer every day to your source(s). Once you gain a comfortability, try out some new prayers and incorporate them into everyday occurrences.

7. A good rule of thumb, if you are not feeling spiritualty around you, you may not be looking in the right place. If you have this block, introduce yourself to new ideas by researching different forms of spirituality. You may want to start with a book, spiritual study group, a house of worship, or a meditation class. Whenever I have found myself at a cross roads with my divine source or blocked, I will go to one of these four to gain new insights and see where I am feeling the pull to dig deeper.

There are three principles to always keep in mind when praying and connecting with *your* source.

1. The first principle is Mathew 7:7, "Ask and you shall receive." It is by divine right that you receive what you ask for. Wording your prayers appropriately is vital. An example of this is, when I was so unwell at 25, I said "Please universe, I don't care what it takes, please get rid of this physical pain and OCD." Divine source responded by removing my ills. It was then replaced it with a much worse

form when I almost died at 31 years old. I have now learned our desires should wholly be up to divine source in divine time. Always let the source guide the way with light, love, protection, peace, strength, and support it offers completely.

2. The second principle is Mark 11:24 which states, "Therefore I tell you, whatever you ask for in prayer, believe that you have received it, and it will be yours." It is important when we are connecting with source, believing this prayer has already been received is imperative. For years, I prayed and talked with my sources and was always finding myself in the continual cycles of life, making no headway. I didn't actually believe these prayers to be real in present tense. It was a lot of wishing, hoping, and trying. It wasn't until I learned through one of my spiritual teachers that we must speak and act as if our prayers are already answered in the present tense and we pour our gratitude out for these offerings we receive.

3. The last principle is to always get quiet and still. When actions are based on chaos, divine will not know how to respond because there is no calmness or clarity. The daily writing and inner confidant are where I learned to get off the highway of chaos and slow down to seek the clarity needed to connect with divine.

Be patient with yourself. All of us will have different paths, timelines, and connections with source. After many years of experimenting, I now pray to multiple sources, multiple times a day to myself and out loud. We are now best friends and do everything together. When I am overwhelmed with gratitude and joy, I speak with my divine guides. When I feel the battles becoming too much to fight alone, I speak with my divine guides. For when we accept divine wholly without judgement, we attract a fully committed and accepting form of pure love back. The beauty of spirituality is within all of us, I pray you too will realize this beauty.

Step 4: Triple Threat

Duration: 1 Week

I always smile when I hear someone say, "I would die for my family. I would take a bullet for them." Yet, this is the same person who wakes up to a large flavored coffee drink ladened with over 200mg of caffeine and 70g of sugar, sits 16 hours a day with a computer and TV, drinks alcohol every night and weekend, consumes over 70% of their diet from ultra processed foods, keeps low level friendships around, and uses synthetic chemicals on and around their body multiple times a day. They are slowly killing themselves and not giving it one thought. Our physical state is the last side of the triangle to address and consists of the triple threat. The triple threat is three components: what we put inside and outside our body, our physical activity, and the company we keep. I bet right now, if it is not you, you know multiple people who have chronic health issues- heart disease, autoimmunity disorders, addictions, anxiety, obesity, diabetes, infertility, etc. Each day our bodies are hit with a borage of toxicities without even batting an eye. These toxicities cause dis-ease. When our triple threat becomes inharmonious, we become inharmonious.

Threat 1: Inside and Outside Our Body

We have been tricked into thinking what we are presented with is "normal". The average American starts their day with a large artificially flavored coffee/tea drink which can have upwards 200mg of caffeine, over 70g (1/3 cup) of sugar, and artificial flavors. The coffee drink is then accompanied with a processed sugary bread for breakfast such as muffin or scone which contains inflammatory seed oils, artificial flavors, preservatives, and another 25g (1/8 cup) of sugar. At lunch, this person may then have a burrito with processed bleached wheat tortilla containing seed oils, preservatives, non-organic vegetables, and meat that has been treated with hormones and/or antibiotics. The day is then ended with a low-quality protein, a non-organic vegetable, a processed starch such as pasta and a few glasses of wine or beer. These foods are filled with sugar, processed lab ingredients, inflammatory seed oils, and more antibiotics, hormones, and pesticides that I think any of us would like to imagine. All of these poor-quality ingredients are proven to expedite many different types of diseases. Humans have been on this planet for thousands of years without all of the processed and chemically charged junk that is thrown in our faces. Currently, infertility rates, autoimmune disorders, mental illnesses, and diabetes are higher than ever before and only continuing to grow. Companies spend millions of dollars to make food and drinks addictive and toxic. It is a science experiment and we are the rat.

The reality is, humans don't need any ultra-processed lab food or drinks to survive. We need it to become addicted and sick which makes these companies more money. By this, I mean, they sell the product that makes us sick and then produce the pharmaceutical for the illness. Without the addiction and illnesses, they're not in business. The masses are happily, freely, and willingly paying these companies to make them sick. Through having to heal family members and myself time and time again, I learned, our greatest source of nutrients for optimal health, physically and mentally, come from real fruit, real vegetables, real meat, real fish, real spices and herbs, real grains, real fat sources such as tallow, butter, or olive oil, and real water. This week, one of your objectives, is to start shopping on the outer rims of the store where the *real* food sits and only eat *real* food. Start reading the back of food and drink labels. Start educating yourself on artificial flavors, artificial colors, pesticides, msg, hormones and antibiotics added to meat, farmed fish, the dirty dozen, added sugars, glyphosate, and GMO's. All of these have been studied and shown to have negative effects on our health. You may want to check out your farmer's market for seasonal local produce and meats. The planet was our only grocery store for thousands of years. There are over 2,000 fruits, over 1,000 vegetables, 21 grains, over 20 nuts, around 1,800 cheeses, over 400 types of beans, numerous types of eggs, countless spices and herbs, many types of fish, and an abundance of poultry and meat options.

To illustrate how our system is set up to fail us, here are a few different examples. The majority of the processed foods and drinks sold in America are sold in other places around the world. How come these countries aren't seeing the same issues as America? The reason is these processed food companies have to change the product ingredients to be cleaner due to the countries stricter ingredient laws. The same exact products sold in American versus around the world have a completely different set of ingredients. Europe, for example, has numerous food additives such as titanium dioxide, brominated vegetable oil, potassium bromate, synthetic foods dyes, and many other ingredients banned. America is also an avid GMO user. We are the highest producer of GMO crops in the world. There are a total of 26 countries which have a total or partial ban on the usage of GMO's. America is also the second biggest user of pesticides. Some pesticides, which are banned worldwide, are still being used in America. These chemicals are in the majority of foods sitting on our tables. At the end of the day, it is not up to them for us to be healthy. It is up to us to become educated and make the change we wish to see for ourselves.

While I became serious about cleaning up my diet after I saw healing take place, I did not take seriously the idea of cleaning up my immediate outer environment. It wasn't until I got sick at 25, when I quickly changed my mind. I started getting headaches and short of breath with any strongly scented smells. Chlorine pools started to make me itch and short of breath for days. Personal care products that weren't naturally derived started giving me rashes. Household cleaning products were making me feel dizzy and short of breath. Moldy places made my OCD worse. Once I had started to do a deep dive into what was causing my OCD, I became educated on all the ingredients my body was having to process every day. Just to put into perspective what was put on my body daily, I listed the chemicals used every day on my body. This list includes one shampoo, one conditioner, one face wash, one body wash, one deodorant, one body lotion, one toothpaste, one nail polish, one tinted moisturizer, one mascara, one clothing detergent, and one perfume. All of these items can be found at most general stores.

1. aqua/water/eau, sodium lauroyl sarcosinate, cocamidopropyl hydroxysultaine, cocamidopropyl betaine, parfum/fragrance, lactamide mea, glycerin, acrylates/palmeth-25 acrylate copolymer, argania spinosa (argan) kernel oil, chondrus crispus extract, ascophyllum nodosum extract, laminaria saccharina extract, palmaria palmata extract, undaria pinnatifida extract, xylitylglucoside, peg-150 pentaerythrityl tetrastearate, anhydroxylitol, sodium pca, styrene/acrylates copolymer, peg-6 caprylic/capric glycerides, citric acid, lauric acid, polyquaternium-7, propylene glycol, xylitol, sodium sarcosinate, tetrasodium edta, polysorbate 20, disodium edta, ethylhexylglycerin, peg-20 glyceryl laurate, glucose, tocopherol, linoleic acid, retinyl palmitate, caprylic/capric triglyceride, diethylhexyl syringylidenemalonate, phenoxyethanol, sodium benzoate, potassium sorbate, chlorphenesin, alpha-isomethyl ionone, linalool, hydroxycitronellal, aqua/water/eau, dimethicone, cetearyl alcohol, parfum/fragrance, behentrimonium chloride, acetamide mea, canola oil, argania spinosa (argan) kernel oil, allium sativum bulb extract, anthemis nobilis flower extract, arctium lappa root extract, arnica montana flower extract, hedera helix (ivy)

extract, lamium album flower extract, nasturtium officinale leaf extract, pinus sylvestris bud extract, rosmarinus officinalis (rosemary) leaf extract, hydrolyzed vegetable protein pg-propyl silanetriol, citric acid, acrylates copolymer, polyquaternium-37, ppg-1 trideceth-6, caprylyl glycol, propylene glycol, sorbitan oleate, propylene glycol dicaprylate/dicaprate, isopropyl alcohol, disodium edta, chlorphenesin, phenoxyethanol, potassium sorbate, alpha-isomethyl ionone, linalool, hydroxycitronellal, water/eau, decyl glucoside, disodium cocoamphodiacetate, cocamidopropyl pg-dimonium chloride phosphate, peg-120 methyl glucose dioleate, ethoxydiglycol, citric acid, dmdm hydantoin, parfum/fragrance, hexamidine diisethionate, water (eau), cocamidopropyl betaine, sodium lauroyl isethionate, sodium methyl lauroyl taurate, sodium chloride, sodium benzoate, glycerin, fragrance (parfum), stearic acid, palmitic acid, hydrogenated vegetable glycerides, glyceryl stearate, glycol distearate, hydroxystearic acid, rosa canina fruit oil, paeonia officinalis flower extract, lauric acid, carrageenan, cyamopsis tetragonoloba (guar) gum, sodium gluconate, citric acid, phenoxyethanol, citronellol, geraniol, hexyl cinnamal, limonene, linalool, red 33 (ci 17200), yellow 5 (ci 19140), aluminum zirconium tetrachlorohydrex gly 18.2%, cyclopentasiloxane, stearyl alcohol, c12 15 alkyl benzoate, ppg 14 butyl ether, hydrogenated castor oil, parfum, dimethicone, polyethylene, caprylic/capric triglyceride, maltodextrin, hydrolyzed corn starch, gelatin crosspolymer, hydrated silica, cellulose gum, sodium starch octenylsuccinate, silica, bht, helianthus annuus (sunflower) seed oil, water, glycerin, alcohol denat., cetearyl alcohol, stearic acid, glyceryl dilaurate, cetyl esters, dimethicone, lanolin oil, fragrance, hydroxyacetophenone, caprylic/capric triglyceride, arginine, sodium hydroxide, acrylates/c10-30 alkyl acrylate crosspolymer, tetrasodium glutamate diacetate, tocopheryl acetate, phenoxyethanol, alpha-isomethyl ionone, amyl cinnamal, benzyl alcohol, benzyl salicylate, cinnamyl alcohol, citronellol, coumarin, eugenol, geraniol, hydroxycitronellal, isoeugenol, limonene, linalool, sodium fluoride (0.16% w/v fluoride ion)(0.243%), glycerin, hydrated silica, sodium hexametaphosphate, water, peg-6, flavor, sodium lauryl sulfate, cocamidopropyl betaine, trisodium phosphate, sodium saccharin, pvp, carrageenan, xanthan gum, sucralose, mica, titanium dioxide, butyl acetate, ethyl acetate, nitrocellulose, tosylamide/epoxy resin, acetyl tributyl citrate, isopropyl alcohol, stearalkonium bentonite, benzophenone-1, silica, trimethylpentanediyl dibenzoate, polyvinyl butyral, barium sulfate, titanium dioxide (ci 77891), red 6 (ci 15850), yellow 5 (ci 19140), octinoxate 6 %, titanium dioxide 5.6 %; other ingredients: water, methyl trimethicone, alcohol, dimethicone, phenyl trimethicone, butylene glycol, talc, isododecane, polymethylsilsesquioxane, acrylates/polytrimethylsiloxymethacrylate copolymer, polymethyl methacrylate, nelumbo nucifera flower water, peg-10 dimethicone, alumina, dimethicone/peg-10/15 crosspolymer, stearic acid, aluminum hydroxide, phenoxyethanol, magnesium sulfate, fragrance, triethoxycaprylylsilane, methylparaben, sodium hyaluronate, tocopheryl acetate, dipropylene glycol, polyurethane-15, bht, laminaria digitata extract, tocopherol, propylparaben, ethylparaben, [+ / - (may contain), ultramarines, iron oxides, titanium dioxide, mica, aqua/water/eau, paraffin, stearic acid, triethanolamine, cera alba/beeswax/cire dabeille, acacia senegal/acacia senegal gum, palmitic acid, cera, carnauba/carnauba wax/cire de carnauba, hydroxyethylcellulose, panthenol, imidazolidinyl urea, sodium polymet, c10-16 pareth, sodium c10-16 alkylbenzenesulfonate, sodium salts of c12-18 fatty acids, propylene glycol, sodium citrate, c10-16 alkyldimethylamine oxide, sodium borate, sodium cumenesulfonate, polyethyleneimine alkoxylated, subtilisin, sodium formate, amylase enzyme, mannanase enzyme, cellulase enzyme, alcohol denat. parfum (fragrance), aqua/water/eau, butyl methoxydibenzoylmethane, propylene glycol, benzyl benzoate, benzyl salicylate, coumarin, hydroxycitronellal, limonene, linalool, blue 1 (ci 42090), red 4 (ci 14700), yellow 5 (ci19140).

And I wonder why I didn't feel well? All of these products and their ingredients came in contact with my skin every day. Our skin is our largest organ and absorbs everything we put on it. Our liver then has to process everything our bodies absorb. Eventually these toxins build up and manifest into illnesses. In this list, there are numerous neurotoxins, heavy metals, endocrine disruptors, etc. My list does not include BPA water bottles or the household cleaners I used regularly. My point is to bring awareness to what we are truly using and know there is sufficient evidence that a lot of these chemicals cause harm. After cleansing my immediate environment of these toxins, my brain fog, rashes, OCD, anxiety, body odor, body aches, shortness of breath, headaches, hormones, joint pains, and so many more symptoms were healing. I could start thinking clearly again. I am now a staunch believer our environment makes up how we physically and mentally feel.

Europe has over 1,300 personal care products ingredients banned. There are only 9 ingredients banned in America. Currently, America has over 80,000 chemicals registered to use. So far, only a few hundred of these have been studied for safety. If you have unexplained symptoms or not feeling or thinking your best, this week start to research. Look into the health implications from household cleaning products, personal hygiene products, BPA water bottles, non-stick cookware, forever chemicals in workout clothing, heavy metals in makeup, toxins in feminine hygiene products, water quality report from your city, proximity to superfund sites, emf's and cell towers, mold in the home, PERC from dry cleaning, artificial chemical fragrances and air fresheners, and VOC's. We are swimming in a toxic soup. Don't underestimate the power of cleaning up what is being used on and around your body. We only get one body in our lifetime, try treating it with the care it deserves.

Threat 2: Physical Movement

The second threat is how we are physically moving our bodies. The average American is sitting over eight hours per day. We are one of a few countries that does not incorporate physical movement into our daily life. Most countries walk to work and the market, garden their own fruits and vegetables, farm animals, spend time in the parks, etc. Most Americans get in a car, sit in traffic, sit at a desk all day, sit in traffic back home, sit at home watching tv, and then sleeps. We have lost total connection with ourselves and moving our bodies. When we embark on a journey of self-rediscovery, moving the physical body is imperative. Without movement, our systems become stagnated and the toxicities and energies cannot leave our body. This ultimately weighs us down. Throughout all of my ups and downs, movement came in some way, shape, or form. Intuitively, I knew I would be even more unwell if I didn't keep up some form of movement. This week I suggest trying one style of workout for 10 minutes each day and see how it resonates. Some ideas are walking, tennis, jujitsu, Pilates, spin, tai chi, strength training, yoga, golf, basketball, soccer, running, swimming, or calisthenics. You can now find almost any type of workout on YouTube for free. I only ask that you make it something you enjoy. I don't believe movement needs to be this tedious activity. I believe we can get movement in a way that is supportive and healthy. Past this week, exercise should be incorporated into every day of your life. It does not need to look the same every day. One day you may walk 10 minutes. Another day you may do a twenty-minute yoga flow or a three-mile run. The most important part is to just move. Your mind and body will thank you.

I learned about a concept that Japan uses called Shirin-Yoku. The layman's term is forest bathing, or immersing yourself completely in nature. Doctors prescribe this as an intervention for depression and other ailments. Studies were conducted and forest bathing was found to be more helpful than the conventional treatments for depression. The plants in nature release a compound called phytoncides. These phytoncides are responsible for killing off cancer activity, lowering cortisol, lowering inflammation, fighting off depressing and anxiety, and improving sleep. In a world where we spend so much time sitting inside and burnt out from the day to day, it's no wonder our rates of physical and mental health issues have risen higher and higher, year after year. Sick building syndrome is now on the rise here in the states. This is where the toxins from inside buildings with no access to fresh air, build up in the body, burden the liver, and cause a whole slew of health issues. This week and beyond, try to spend at least 30 minutes outside per day. You may want to try incorporating your daily movement outside when possible.

When looking around, all of the plants and animals tunefully listen, rely on, and work with nature. Bears hibernate, butterflies migrate, flowers go dormant for winter and bloom in spring, plants absorb carbon dioxide and release oxygen, and the moon and sun dance around the earth every day. It is never too late for us to get back with nature as intended and live in alignment. Mother nature has everything we need to survive. When our bare feet touch the ground, the soil is scientifically proven to heal us. This happens through the exchange of electrons with our body's electric charge and the earths electric charge. Mother nature has an abundance of herbs that can heal many ailments. She has the sunset trances for deeper meaning and the sunrises for hopeful new beginnings. Her moon cycle is linked to women's cycles and men's sleep pattern. Women generally ovulate with a full moon or new moon, while men will sleep better on average 20 minutes longer during the waning and waxing phases of the moon. Her sun gives us the strength and immunity, in the form of Vitamin D, needed to fight off illnesses. Her elements have the capacity to keep us in place to rest or propel us to a higher calling. Allow yourself the privilege of letting the wind, grass, sun, birds, rain, moon, water, mountains, and animals nourish your soul. You may discover you are able to tap into a different side of yourself in this setting. Get back to her and you might find your prayers answered, your soul hugged, and your heart full.

Threat 3: Company We Keep

Our final threat is the company we surround ourselves with. This is the friends, family, romantic partners, acquaintances, or co-workers we engage with on a daily basis. Throughout this playbook, most people will see their relationships pop up and start to see them from their point of view again. Sometimes, the truth of these relationships starts to become apparent which may be heartbreaking and scary or on the other hand, comforting and exciting. Biologically, were social beings and are wired to be with people. I believe it is in our innate nature to want to keep relationships even under undesirable circumstances. Maybe this is a survival mechanism so were not left "alone". The reality is some relationships aren't worth saving while others are worth preserving. Only you will be able to make this distinction. Relationships have the power to take us down or build us up, choosing wisely is imperative. Keep in mind, if we keep a low-level relationship alive, we will fall to them, they won't rise to us.

In order to decipher where you stand with your relationships, use this exercise for each of your relationships with close friends, family, work partners, acquaintances, and romantic partners.

1. Grab a sheet of paper and draw a line down the center of the page.
2. On the left side of the line, write down the qualities you desire in someone for this particular relationship.
3. On the right side of the line, for each quality you wrote, write down the quality you need to assume or express in order to attract this type of person.

There are two reasons why this exercise is important. First, it shows us what we are really looking for in a relationship. Usually, this highlights what we have been putting up with for far too long. Second, by defining the person you need to become, it will allow you to take action on those qualities and make intentional change to attract what you seek. Seneca said, "Nothing, however, delights the mind as much as loving and loyal friendship." Friendship will bring peace, comfort, and a warm relentless support. The mind should not suffer and become dark under a pure connection. If you keep a poisonous relationship, the venom tends to spread which may manifest into physical, mental, and spiritual illnesses. During seasons of growth and self-renewal, there seems to always be one person in the sphere that starts to shame, question, or stop us from achieving anything greater. This behavior is usually a form of criticization and insecurity in order for them to either feel better about themselves, stop you from achieving more than them, or so they don't lose the person they've always known. When this happens, bless this person silently as they are usually in a greater pain than we may realize and then move aside to let them pass by freely while you continue to grow. Try keeping tabs on those who stuck by you during times of renewal. Someone who is happy for you or doing better than you will never criticize you for your efforts. During your daily writing, a continual check-in on your relationships will help keep you defined on where you stand with them, with yourself, and when it is time to let them go or nurture them to grow.

Essentially, we take on the characteristics of our surroundings. When we consume dead processed foods, we become dead. When we swallow alcohol, it swallows our judgement, emotions, and goals. When we are swimming in a toxic soup of chemicals thinking were invincible, the universe always has its way of humbling us. When we surround ourselves with people who use gossip as currency, use our weaknesses for their strength, and act on negativity and judgment, we will inevitably become that type of person. By taking the initiative to slowly become aware and defining the highest self for the highest good, we are taking the first step in essential liberation.

Step 5: Plan with a Purpose

Duration: 1 Week

What is the purpose of all this if we don't have a purpose? By the time you get to this step, my hope is many things. First, the daily writing has allowed you to let go, even if it is just a little, and see yourself and the world around you more clearly. Second, the inner critic is now your inner confidant and best friend pushing you daily to the heights you deserve. Third, your wisdom is built and used through the power of having faith and letting that faith guide your path. Lastly, your physical body and environment are starting to work harmoniously at keeping you healthy and safe. We must travel through these steps to remove the dense fog and see the future we desire. Once we've reached the top of the pyramid, we are now being pointed in the right direction, the direction of the highest self. The future of us relies on the current reality we create. It relies on self-awareness, accountability, inner knowing's, deeper wisdom, and a willingness to take action for the greater good. Without these substantial qualities, most of us follow a path with a lack of meaning, lack of value, or lack to persevere. These attributes stop the mind from achieving all it can accomplish. Most of us have big dreams that are never fulfilled and feel like just that, a dream. The reason for this is because most people don't know exactly what they want and the steps it will take to get there. I will show you how to harness the ideas and goals and begin building the purposeful life you deserve. If you can create something in your mind, you can create it in your life.

If we don't make goals for ourselves, we will get stuck in everyone else's goals around us. I would always let life happen to me, instead of, for me. When my autoimmune flare up happened and I wasn't sure I was going to make it, I got very serious with my goals. I realized at that moment I didn't want my journey to end there without the dreams I truly had for myself. This is where I started to tinker with different ideas on how to generate a plan for successful goal making. Eventually, I came up with a two-step process. The first step starts with a physical, tangible vision of the goals such as a vision board and the second step is to pick one goal at a time and systematically work through that particular goal. Before you start on these next exercises, there is an important lesson I learned. Do NOT share your goals with others. I've witnessed goal sharing being one of the biggest blocks to completing the goal. It leaves the door open for commentary, interpretation, and a sense of false completion. To start making forward movement, treat goal setting as any other individual activity.

Most people cannot see the vision because they simply just don't know who they are and what they want. But you do. You've been doing all this work on yourself through daily writing, positive affirmations, creating faith, and cultivating a harmonious environment, inside and out. The first exercise to propel you on your path is a vision board. The board puts the imaginary world into tangible form. This is the first step in turning a dream into a reality.

1. Buy a board. You can use any type of board such as a poster board, a tri-fold board, or a leftover box that has been opened up to be flat.
2. Gather pictures, words, objects or anything that has meaning to your vision for your future. These images or items could come from the computer, a book, magazine, personal photos, etc. Some examples to put on the board are career, business, hobbies, marriage, purpose, physical health, self-growth, emotional goals, intellectual goals, family, cars, houses, pets, friendships, spirituality, etc. Nothing is too superficial, too emotional, or too intellectual to put on here. It could be as metaphorical or exact as you want. There is no right or wrong way to make this. Create your visions based off of the deep belief in these particular goals. Remember, this is for you and only you.
    a. It is important to note, when you are choosing your goals for the board, check-in with yourself for each goal and see how it is making you feel. Goals should be bringing a sense of peace and excitement. Over the years, I've witnessed many people's goals bring a sense of urgency, fear, or volatility. If this is the case, this is not your authentic goal. Make sure this is not your friends' goals, your families' goals, your partners goals, or your role models goals infiltrating your path. Make sure you're doing something because you want, not out

of fear that someone else has what you don't. This is a form of jealousy and should be avoided at all costs. By living in this state, you will never get ahead because the person you're trying to be will always be one step ahead of you. Intentionally sit with each goal and make sure it's a path of purity, peace, excitement, and joy.

3. Start to glue or tape on all of the items in a way that feels right to you. It can be in rows or scattered. There could be certain sections for each aspect of your life or there could be an emotion guiding the board. We all think and create different. Be as creative or pragmatic as you'd like.

4. Set this board up where you will see it the most. Let it marinate in your mind and act as a reminder when things start to go astray. I put mine where I wake up and fall asleep. I let the images and ideas spark joy in the morning and be my lullaby at night. Every season, I revisit my board to see if there are any shifts or changes.

Once you are finished with this board there may be a wide range of emotions and thoughts. It can be overwhelming. Witness these and let them pass. This board is just a motivation and a point of guidance for you. The pictures will lead to the next exercise of putting goals into action and the steps it will take to obtain these goals. I call this next exercise the baby steps checklist.

1. Take a sheet of paper.
2. Look at your vision board and pick a single goal that is either intuitively jumping at you the loudest or one you

believe will make the biggest impact for your future once completed.

3. Write this goal down on the bottom of the page.
4. At the top of the page, write down where you are right now pertaining to this goal.
5. In between where you are now and your goal, make a numbered, detailed list of each baby step it will take to get to this goal. The more detailed you are here, the higher chance of success you have at achieving the goal. Now is a great time to reacquaint yourself with your strengths and weaknesses you worked on in step one. Use these to your advantage to get where you want to go.
6. Carry this checklist with you at all times and review it every day to stay on track and in the present. Each time you accomplish one of the baby steps, check it off. Continue doing this until you've reached your goal.
7. Once you reach your goal, start a new checklist for the next goal.

The checklist may seem trivial at first, yet it will keep you organized and in line with yourself, your accomplishments, and the work you still need to do. Once the momentum of baby steps takes hold, you will start to think better, feel better, and do better.

These two exercises are the gentle daily reminder on WHY we need to keep going, HOW we are going to get there, and WHAT it will take to accomplish the dream we all have living inside. These goals keep us grounded and focused so there is nowhere to stray.

Sincerely,

Socrates said, "The unexamined life is not worth living." It is much easier to stay on course when these steps are consciously practiced. By continually reassessing and living in these five steps of the pyramid, you will embody your most authentic highest being; A life fully dictated by you. There are two games in life. The short game and the long game. The short game is grabbing onto anyone or anything for achievement, comparison, worth, or direction. This game is immediate, self-gratification and will always leave you depleted in the end. The long game is a continual recalibration of self for grounding, inward achievement, growth, and purpose. This game is slower and at times tougher, but always more fulfilling in the end. You carry the innate power to change the course. Now is the time to harness the power of the long game to cultivate a life worth living. Cherish the highs and thank the lows. Both will take you exactly where you're meant to go. Try not letting the over thinking cloud your emotions or your over feeling cloud your thinking. Keep walking through the open doors and let the closed ones pass freely. We only get one shot at life, best make it an authentic one.

www.ingramcontent.com/pod-product-compliance
Lightning Source LLC
Chambersburg PA
CBHW032053040426
42449CB00007B/1102